SUPER SIMPLE

CHRISTMAS

ACTIVITIES

❖ FUN AND EASY HOLIDAY PROJECTS FOR KIDS ❖

Megan Borgert-Spaniol

Consulting Editor, Diane Craig, M.A./Reading Specialist

Super Sandcastle

An Imprint of Abdo Publishing
abdopublishing.com

abdopublishing.com

Published by Abdo Publishing, a division of ABDO, PO Box 398166, Minneapolis, Minnesota 55439.
Copyright © 2018 by Abdo Consulting Group, Inc. International copyrights reserved in all countries.
No part of this book may be reproduced in any form without written permission from the publisher.
Super SandCastle™ is a trademark and logo of Abdo Publishing.

Printed in the United States of America, North Mankato, Minnesota

102017
012018

 THIS BOOK CONTAINS RECYCLED MATERIALS

Design: Alison Stuerman, Mighty Media, Inc.
Production: Mighty Media, Inc.
Editor: Rebecca Felix
Cover Photographs: Mighty Media, Inc.; Shutterstock
Interior Photographs: Mighty Media, Inc.; Shutterstock

The following manufacturers/names appearing in this book are trademarks: Artist's Loft™,
Cake Mate®, Craft Smart®, Elmer's®, Elmer's® Glue-All™, Franklin Sports®, Mod Podge®,
Scotch®, Sharpie®

Publisher's Cataloging-in-Publication Data
Names: Borgert-Spaniol, Megan, author.
Title: Super simple Christmas activities: fun and easy holiday projects for kids /
by Megan Borgert-Spaniol.
Other titles: Fun and easy holiday projects for kids
Description: Minneapolis, Minnesota : Abdo Publishing, 2018. | Series: Super simple holidays |
Identifiers: LCCN 2017946522 | ISBN 9781532112430 (lib.bdg.) | ISBN 9781614799856 (ebook)
Subjects: LCSH: Christmas decorations--Juvenile literature. | Handicraft--Juvenile literature. |
Holiday decorations--Juvenile literature.
Classification: DDC 745.59412--dc23
LC record available at https://lccn.loc.gov/2017946522

Super SandCastle™ books are created by a team of professional educators, reading specialists,
and content developers around five essential components—phonemic awareness, phonics,
vocabulary, text comprehension, and fluency—to assist young readers as they develop reading
skills and strategies and increase their general knowledge. All books are written, reviewed,
and leveled for guided reading and early reading intervention for use in shared, guided, and
independent reading and writing activities to support a balanced approach to literacy instruction.

TO ADULT HELPERS

The craft projects in this series are fun and simple. There are just a few things to remember to keep kids safe. Some projects require the use of sharp objects. Also, kids may be using messy materials such as glue or paint. Make sure they protect their clothes and work surfaces. Review the projects before starting and be ready to assist when necessary.

KEY SYMBOL

Watch for this warning symbol in this book. Here is what it means.

SHARP!

 You will be working with a sharp object. Get help!

CONTENTS

HAPPY HOLIDAYS!

Holidays are great times to celebrate with family and friends. Many people have favorite holiday **traditions**. Some traditions are hundreds of years old. But people start new traditions too, such as making holiday foods and crafts.

CHRISTMAS

Christmas is a **Christian** holiday. It is the celebration of the birth of **Jesus Christ**. Christians celebrate Christmas all around the world.

Christians in many countries celebrate this holiday on December 25. Some countries use a different calendar. Christians in these countries celebrate Christmas on January 7.

CELEBRATE CHRISTMAS

Several Christmas **traditions** are common throughout many countries. Do you celebrate using any of these traditions?

EVERGREEN TREES

Around 1600, German **Christians** began decorating evergreen trees at Christmas. The tradition spread to other countries in the 1800s. Today, families worldwide decorate evergreen trees at Christmas using ornaments, lights, and more.

CHRISTMAS WREATHS

For **Christians**, the circular shape of evergreen wreaths represents the life story of **Jesus Christ**. Wreaths are **symbols** of the joy and peace of the Christmas season.

SANTA CLAUS

Santa Claus is known by many names. Saint Nicholas and Kris Kringle are two. No matter what he is called, Santa represents the spirit of Christmas. He is a fun holiday **tradition** for many families!

7

MATERIALS

Here are some of the materials that you will need for the projects in this book.

ACRYLIC PAINT

BANANAS AND STRAWBERRIES

BLUE TRI-FOLD PROJECT BOARD

BOTTLE CAPS

BOWL

BUTTONS

CARD STOCK

CHENILLE STEMS

CHOCOLATE SPRINKLES

CINNAMON CANDIES

COLORED PAPER

CRAFT GLUE

CRAFT KNIFE

FESTIVE WRAPPING PAPER

GLITTER

GLUE STICK

JEWELS

MARKERS

MARSHMALLOWS (LARGE & MINI)

MOD PODGE DIMENSIONAL MAGIC

OLD CHRISTMAS CARDS

PING-PONG BALLS

RIBBON

RULER

SCISSORS

STRING

TAPE

TOOTHPICKS

WHITE PAPER

WOODEN CRAFT STICKS

BUTTON ORNAMENT CARD

Create a custom Christmas card to celebrate the season!

MERRY CHRISTMAS!

WHAT YOU NEED

card stock, 8.5" × 11"

ruler

markers

scissors

buttons

craft glue

1 Measure 7½ inches (19 cm) along the long edge of the card stock. Draw a vertical line at the mark.

2 Cut the card stock along the line. Fold the larger piece in half **lengthwise**.

3 Write "Merry Christmas" or another holiday saying on the front of the card.

4 Glue on the button ornaments. Let the glue dry.

5 Draw a string and bow from the top of the card to each ornament.

6 Write a holiday message inside your card. Then give it to someone to wish them a Merry Christmas!

TIP You can mail your card to a friend or family member! It fits in a #10 envelope.

BRIGHT LIGHTS

Create a string of colorful bulbs
to brighten any room!

WHAT YOU NEED

marker

card stock

scissors

colored paper

ruler

glue stick

tape

string

toothpick

12

1 Draw a bulb shape on the card stock. Cut it out. This is the bulb **template**.

2 Trace the bulb template on colored paper. Repeat to make 10 to 20 bulbs of different colors. Cut the bulbs out.

3 Cut a long strip of black paper 2 inches (5 cm) wide. Fold it in half **lengthwise**.

4 Cut a piece of the folded strip as wide as one bulb base. Repeat for all the bulbs.

5 Put glue along both edges of a bulb base. Fold a black strip over the base. Leave space between the fold and the top of the base. Let the glue dry. Repeat for all bulbs.

6 Tape one end of the string to a toothpick. Pull the toothpick and string through the space between each fold and bulb base. Remove the toothpick from the string.

7 Hang your **garland** for holiday cheer!

BANANA SANTAS

Have fresh fruit fun with these sweet treats!

WHAT YOU NEED

strawberries
sharp knife
cutting board
large marshmallows
bananas
wooden skewers
mini marshmallows
chocolate sprinkles
cinnamon candies

14

1 Rinse the strawberries. Have an adult help you cut off the leaves and stems to make flat ends.

2 Have an adult help you cut each large marshmallow into three **slices**.

3 Peel the bananas. Cut each banana into three pieces.

4 Slide a banana piece onto one end of a skewer. Add a marshmallow slice. Add a strawberry. Top with a mini marshmallow.

5 Place chocolate sprinkles on the bananas for the eyes. Use cinnamon candies for the noses. Then enjoy your Santa treats!

TABLETOP SNOWBALL TOSS

Have a ball with this cool Christmas game!

WHAT YOU NEED

white paper
scissors
ruler
pencil
glue stick
blue tri-fold
  project board
craft knife
colored paper
ping-pong balls

16

1 Lay a sheet of paper on the table. Fold one short edge so it lines up with a long edge. This makes a triangle. Cut off the strip next to the triangle.

2 Place the triangle so the fold is at the bottom. Fold the right point over to the left point. **Crease** the fold.

3 Turn the paper so the long edge is at the top. Fold the right side two-thirds of the way to the left side. The point should stick up above the top edge.

(continued on next page)

4 Fold the left side over so it lines up with the right side.

5 Turn the paper over. Cut along the top straight edge to remove the points.

6 Draw a curved line at least 1 inch (2.5 cm) from the point. Cut the point off at the curved line. This will make a hole for the ping-pong ball to go through in the middle of the snowflake.

7 Cut out small shapes along the edges of the triangle. Try small triangles and half circles. Every snowflake is different! Unfold the paper to see how yours turned out.

8 Repeat steps 1 through 7 to make two more snowflakes with large center holes.

9 Make more snowflakes for decoration. These do not need large holes, so skip step 6.

10 Glue all the snowflakes to the project board. Glue down the three with large holes first. Glue the snowflakes from step 9 all around them.

11 Have an adult help you cut holes in the project board to match each large snowflake's center hole.

12 Use colored paper to make trees and a snowperson. Decorate the bottom of the project board with these figures.

13 Time to play! Take turns throwing the ping-pong balls into the snowflake holes.

8

10

11

19

YOU'RE THE ANGEL ORNAMENT

Let your smile add some sparkle to your Christmas tree!

WHAT YOU NEED

colored card stock

bowl

pencil

scissors

ruler

ribbon

metallic chenille
   stem

clear tape

craft glue

photo of you

decorative
   materials,
   such as glitter
   & jewels

1 Trace around the bowl on the card stock. Cut out the circle. Cut the circle in half.

2 Cut a 6-inch (15 cm) piece of ribbon. Fold it in half. Tape the ends to the center of one half circle. The **loop** should stick up above the card stock's straight edge.

3 Fold one end of a chenille stem into a loop. Bend the loop over to form a **halo**. Tape the chenille stem over the ribbon. The halo should stick up above the straight edge.

4 Roll the half circle into a cone. Tape its **seam**.

5 Fold the other half circle in half. Draw a wing shape along the fold. Cut it out. Unfold and glue the wings onto the cone.

6 Cut your face out of the photo. Glue it to the top of the cone. Let the glue dry.

7 Decorate your angel however you like. Then hang it on your Christmas tree!

3

4

5

HANDPRINT WREATH

Hang a handmade wreath of leaves and holly berries!

WHAT YOU NEED

marker

plate

card stock

bowl, smaller than the plate

scissors

lightweight cardboard

2 or 3 shades of green paper

craft glue

red pom-poms

ribbon

red paper

1 Trace the plate on the card stock. Trace the bowl within this circle.

2 Cut out both circles. The card stock ring is the wreath base.

3 Trace your hand on the cardboard. Cut it out. This makes a **template**.

4 Trace the template 20 to 25 times on green paper. Cut out the green hands.

(continued on next page)

23

5 Glue the first hand to one side of the wreath circle. The fingers should point up. Do not glue the fingers.

6 Glue the next hand so it is slightly below the first. Place it so the fingers point slightly in or out.

7 Repeat step 6 to glue the other hands around the wreath circle.

8 Glue red pom-poms in groups of three around the wreath. These are **holly** berries.

9 Tie a piece of ribbon around the top of the wreath to make a hanger.

10 Cut a bow out of red paper. Glue it over the ribbon at the top of the wreath. Then hang your wreath from a door or window!

TIP Instead of making a paper bow, try using a gift bow! Use any color bow you like.

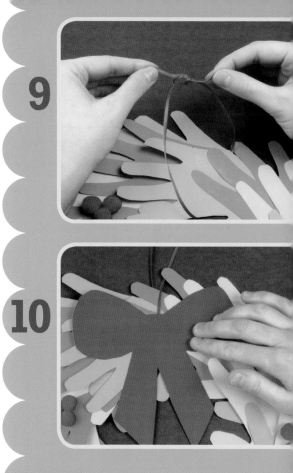

MINI CHRISTMAS TREES

Craft teeny triangle trees to decorate your bigger evergreen!

WHAT YOU NEED

newspaper

wooden craft sticks

acrylic paint in several colors

foam brush

craft glue

ruler

scissors

string

decorative materials, such as chenille stems & jewels

1 Cover your work surface with newspaper. Paint three craft sticks for each tree you want to make. Let the paint dry.

2 Glue two of the sticks together to make the top point of the tree.

3 Cut 2 inches (5 cm) off a third stick. Glue the longer piece across the bottom of the tree.

4 Glue one end of the 2-inch (5 cm) piece to the base of the triangle to make the tree trunk. Let the glue dry.

5 Cut a 5-inch (13 cm) piece of string. Tie it around the top of the tree.

6 Decorate the tree however you like!

7 Repeat steps 2 through 6 to make more ornaments. Then hang them on your holiday tree!

CHRISTMAS MAGNETS

Construct cheery magnets to hang Christmas cards on the fridge!

WHAT YOU NEED

bottle caps

card stock

pencil

scissors

festive wrapping paper, scrapbook paper, or old Christmas cards

craft glue

Mod Podge Dimensional Magic

magnets

1 Place a bottle cap upside down on the card stock. Trace the bottle cap.

2 Cut out the circle. This makes a **template**.

3 Trace the template on **festive** wrapping paper, scrapbook paper, or old Christmas cards. Try tracing the circles around holiday characters, words, or **symbols**. Cut the circles out.

4 Glue a circle inside each bottle cap. Let the glue dry.

5 Fill each bottle cap with Mod Podge Dimensional Magic. Let the Mod Podge dry for at least 3 hours.

6 Glue a magnet to the back of each bottle cap. Let the glue dry.

7 Stick your completed Christmas magnets to your fridge!

29

SLED ORNAMENT

Make a Christmas memory
with a personalized mini sled!

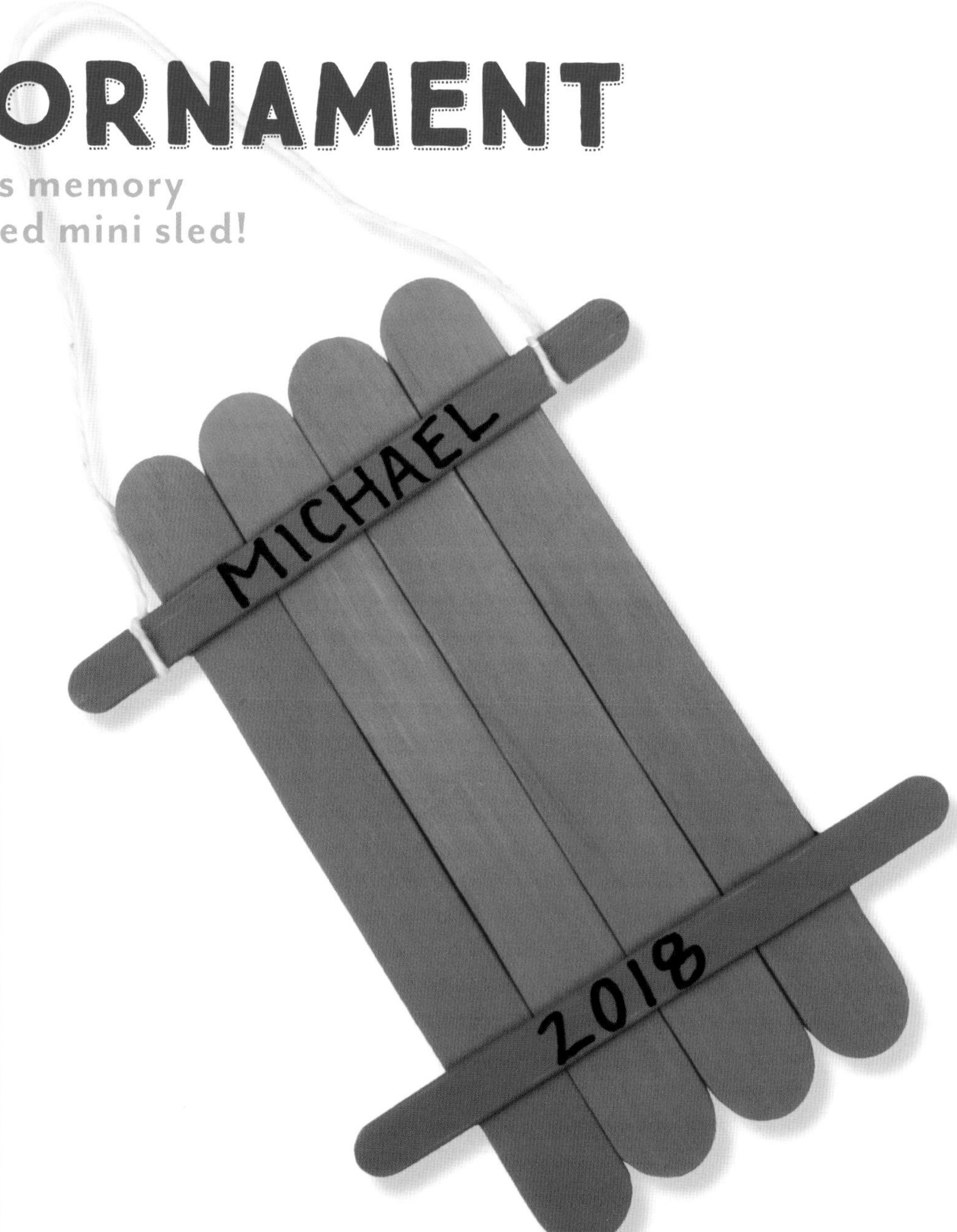

WHAT YOU NEED

newspaper

wooden craft sticks,
    wide and narrow

red & green
    acrylic paint

foam brush

craft glue

ruler

scissors

string

marker

1 Cover your work surface with newspaper. Paint four wide craft sticks red. Paint two narrow craft sticks green. Let the paint dry.

2 Lay the red sticks side by side to make the sled.

3 Glue a green stick across the sled near the top.

4 Glue the other green stick across the sled near the bottom. Let the glue dry.

5 Cut an 8-inch (20 cm) piece of string. Tie its ends to the top green stick's ends.

6 Write your name and the year on your sled. Then hang it on your Christmas tree!

TIP Give your sled as a gift! Write the **recipient**'s name on the sled instead of yours.

GLOSSARY

Christian – having to do with the religion Christianity.

crease – to make a sharp line in something by folding it.

festive – cheerful, bright, and exciting.

garland – a decorative ring or rope made of leaves, flowers, or some other material.

halo – a circle of light shown around the heads of angels or sacred people in artwork.

holly – a type of tree or shrub with evergreen leaves and red berries.

Jesus Christ – the person Christians believe was the son of God.

lengthwise – in the direction of the longest side.

loop – a circle made by a rope, string, or thread.

recipient – a person who receives something.

seam – the line where two edges meet.

slice – a thin piece cut from something.

symbol – an object or picture that stands for or represents something.

template – a shape or pattern that is drawn or cut around to make the same shape in another material.

tradition – a belief or practice passed through a family or group of people.